SUMMARY OF ENTANGLED LIFE

By

Merlin Sheldrake

How Fungi Make Our Worlds, Change our Minds and Shape Our Futures

BlinkRead

GW00394310

BlinkRead

Copyright(c) 2020

Table of Content

BlinkRead

DISCLAIMER:

This book is a summary of Entangled Life; How Fungi Make Our Worlds, Change our Minds and Shape Our Futures By Merlin Sheldrake. It is meant to be a companion, not a replacement, to the original book. Please note that this summary is not authorized, licensed, approved, or endorsed by the author or publisher of the main book. The author of this summary is wholly responsible for the content of this summary and is not associated with the original author or publisher of the main book.

SYNOPSIS:

Entangled Life (2020) ushers us into the vast, hidden world of fungi. In it, we follow molds, yeasts, lichens, and many other fungi as they creep through the soil, intoxicate us with their scent, and induce mesmerizing visions. With a change in perspective, we can begin to see the world from a more fungal point of view −☐ and understand how these organisms might be the key to our future survival.

ABOUT AUTHOR:

Merlin Sheldrake is a fungal biologist with a PhD in tropical ecology from Cambridge University. His research focuses primarily on fungal biology and the history of Amazonian ethnobotany. He is also a musician, brewer, and fermenter.

WHAT'S IN IT FOR ME? EXPLORE THE STRANGE AND MYSTERIOUS WORLD OF FUNGI.

What comes to mind when you hear the word "fungi?" Almost assuredly, it's the mushroom, an organism both reviled and revered around the world. But fungi are so much more.

At this moment, fungi are navigating the dense labyrinths of soil underneath our feet. They are devouring countless materials. They are providing cures for deadly illnesses, and, at the same time, decimating some of humanity's most important crops.

Fungi play a vital role in life on Earth – and yet they're a neglected kingdom, less frequently studied than animals or plants. These read place fungi at center stage as we explore their world and the relationships they've cultivated over millions of years.

Along the way, you'll find out

How fungi can find their way around Tokyo;
what happens when a fungus possesses an
ant; and
Whether fungi are capitalists or socialists.

FUNGI CHALLENGE OUR CONCEPTIONS OF INTELLIGENCE AND INDIVIDUALITY.

The slime mold Physarum polycephalum is a deft problem-solver. When faced with a labyrinth, it's able to compare different courses of action and determine the most efficient way out.

In one experiment, Japanese researchers placed Physarum in petri dishes modeled on the Greater Tokyo area. Oat flakes, which the fungus could use as food, were used to mark out major urban hubs, while harmful bright lights signified obstacles like mountains. After just one day, the slime mold figured out the quickest route among the oat flakes. Remarkably, its network resembled Tokyo's existing rail system almost identically.

Physarum is able to navigate its surroundings and make decisions despite having no brain or central nervous system. Does that mean it lacks intelligence? Or could it be that Physarum and other fungi do possess intelligence —□ just a completely different kind of intelligence from humans?

The key message here is: Fungi challenge our conceptions of intelligence and individuality.

Fungi are a form of network-based life, made up of a collection of thin tubes called hyphae. When hyphae grow, branch, and tangle, they form the dense network known as mycelium. But hyphae also form into fruiting bodies like mushrooms. Slice open a mushroom and you're looking at the very same material that makes up the rest of the mycelium. Often, the purpose of these fruiting bodies is to disperse reproductive spores.

Sounds pretty simple. But try to answer this question: Are mycelial networks individuals or collectives?

On one hand, we can view each mycelial network as a swarm of hyphal tips. Each tip operates individually; there is no leader or central command center. Yet, at the same time, all hyphal tips are connected to one another —□ you can't dismantle a mycelial network hypha by hypha. Reduce a mycelium to just one thin tube and it can regenerate the entire network. This means mycelium is at once a single entity and a multitude of individuals.

Why might this matter to us humans? After all, it's easy for us to define our individual selves. We end where our bodies end, right?

Well, not quite. Our bodies contain entire communities of bacteria, microbes, genes, and cells obtained or inherited from disparate sources. Without them, we'd become sick or even die. Perhaps we, like fungi, are living communities, at once individual and collective. And perhaps it's time we reevaluated our time-honored notions of individuality, autonomy, and self.

FUNGI COMMUNICATE WITH HUMANS, ANIMALS, AND PLANTS THROUGH SCENT.

The smell of truffles is intoxicating. It's heady, pungent, and slightly sweet. Head to a fancy restaurant and you might be lucky enough to have truffles grated over your plate for you — □ in exchange for a pretty penny. Thanks to their rarity, two kilograms' worth of Piedmont white truffles can fetch 12,000 Euros.

For most of the year, truffles exist as underground mycelia. But there comes a time when they must reproduce. They can't do that underground, where there are no air currents or animals to disperse their spores. So truffles must find a way above ground. For this, they release their signature irresistible aroma —□ and soon, animals and humans come to unearth them. Through smell, truffles speak in a language understood by all.

Here's the key message: Fungi communicate with humans, animals, and plants through scent.

Truffles' scents have specifically evolved to enthrall animals. Bears toss logs to the side in order to find the fungi. Elk dig so intently for them that they bloody their noses. And when it comes to humans, truffles are often associated with sex. The word "truffle" actually translates to "testicle" in many languages.

But even before a truffle lures in a bear, elk, or human, it depends on seduction in order to survive.

First, truffle hyphae attract other hyphae to create a mycelial network. Then, it's thought that truffle mycelia release pheromones that entice other fungi to mate with them −□ to fuse together and combine their genetic material. The product of this union is the truffle.

Next, the young truffle must find a plant to partner with – it can't make the carbon compounds it needs to survive on its own. To do this, fungal hyphae and plants engage in a chemical dance of call-and-response. Plant roots produce compounds that cause truffle spores to sprout and hyphae to grow faster. Fungal compounds respond by causing plant roots to expand into feathery branches. This courtship ritual is designed to increase the likelihood of root tips and fungal hyphae joining together.

When truffles are ready to reproduce, they release the chemical cocktail that represents their signature aroma. These seem to arise as a result of complex relationships between a truffle and its unique community of microbes, soil, and climate conditions.

Most of the time, fungal seduction rituals go unnoticed. But when a truffle does release a scent our noses can detect, there is little we can do but heed its call.

LICHENS ARE LIVING EXAMPLES OF WHAT IS BIOLOGICALLY POSSIBLE ON EARTH.

Very few organisms can withstand the extreme environment of outer space. A few can survive if shielded from the sun's harmful radiation. One curious organism, however, lives on even when exposed directly to the most dangerous cosmic rays. That organism is lichen.

Lichen can survive in many extreme environments – not just space. They reside in both scorching deserts and frigid tundras. And they are remarkable in other ways, too – they can be resuscitated after ten years of dehydration, and some species can live for thousands of years.

Lichens' many unique characteristics have made them a darling of biological research, especially in astrobiology. Through lichen, scientists can test the very limits of terrestrial life.

This is the key message: Lichens are living examples of what is biologically possible on Earth.

Lichens have a deep history of disrupting and challenging scientific orthodoxy. In 1869, the Swiss botanist Simon Schwendener proposed the radical idea that lichens may not be a single organism. Instead, he argued that they were a combination of an alga and a fungus, with the alga supplying carbon and the fungus providing protection and nutrients.

At first, Schwendener's hypothesis was firmly rebuked in the scientific community. One scientist even dismissed it as "sensational romance." After all, Darwin's theory of evolution, published in 1859, explained that organisms evolved by diverging from one another. So how could lichens have evolved by converging, as Schwendener proposed?

Over time, Schwendener's theory began to gain more widespread acceptance. However, it wasn't until 1877 that German botanist Albert Frank coined a word —□ symbiosis —□ to describe the exact nature of the relationship between a lichen's algal and fungal components.

Symbiosis is now a widely accepted biological principle. It refers to any sort of partnership between organisms, whether it's mutually beneficial, parasitic, or somewhere in the middle. More than that, the principle of symbiosis transformed scientific understanding. It gave rise, for instance, to American biologist Lynn Margulis's revolutionary theory of endosymbiosis. Margulis argued that multicellular organisms actually evolved by forming symbiotic relationships with unicellular organisms.

Lichen and their symbiosis have forced us to reconsider life in yet more ways. One scientist, Trevor Goward, has actually coined his own term for it: the "lichening rod effect." This describes lichens' tendency to smash conventional insight into pieces and force us to consider new possibilities. Through lichen, we learn more about life itself.

CHEMICALS IN FUNGI HAVE THE POWER TO ALTER HUMAN AND ANIMAL MINDS.

For a few days of its life, the fungus Ophiocordyceps unilateralis possesses the body of an ant.

Yes, you heard that right. Ophiocordyceps is known as a zombie fungus, for its ability to hijack and control the body of an insect. First, Ophiocordyceps infects a carpenter ant, growing into as much as 40 percent of the ant's biomass. The ant loses its fear of heights and begins to climb up a nearby plant. Eventually, the fungus forces the ant to clamp its jaws onto the plant's stem. Mycelium begin to grow from the ant's feet and head, from which bursts a stalk. The stalk releases spores that fall down to ants passing below. And so the cycle continues.

Interestingly, Ophiocordyceps doesn't control the carpenter ant by infecting its brain. Instead, it secretes chemicals that act on the ant's muscle fibers and central nervous system, becoming something like a prosthetic organ. Ophiocordyceps is but one of many examples of fungi manipulating the behavior of other organisms.

The key message here is: Chemicals in fungi have the power to alter human and animal minds.

Ophiocordyceps fungus is closely related to ergot fungi, from which the psychoactive chemical LSD is derived. But ergot fungi aren't the only ones that produce mind-altering chemicals. So, too, do fungi containing psilocybin, a psychedelic substance that's been venerated in human cultures for millennia.

The use of psychoactive mushrooms has been especially well-documented in Central America. In Mexico, for instance, psychedelic "flesh of the gods" mushrooms were served at the Aztec emperor's coronation in 1486.

More recently, psilocybin has been the subject of extensive scientific research. Various studies have concluded that treatment with psilocybin can greatly reduce psychological symptoms associated with depression, anxiety, and even addiction.

Ophiocordyceps uses chemicals to hijack an insect's body and take control in a way that benefits the fungus. Are psychoactive mushrooms perhaps doing the same with human minds −☐ hijacking them so we continue to consume them and spread their spores?

Not exactly. Fungi have been producing psilocybin for tens of millions of years – long before our hominid ancestors evolved. That's far from zombie fungi like Ophiocordyceps, which is completely dependent on the carpenter ant for its life cycle. The evolutionary purpose of psilocybin is still unclear. But without a doubt, these curious mind-altering fungi benefit from the human fascination with the strange visions, egoless states, and euphoria we experience if we ingest them.

MYCORRHIZAL RELATIONSHIPS ARE THE BEDROCK OF LIFE ON EARTH.

Six hundred million years ago, the world was a very different place. The land was barren and scorched −□ no plants or trees yet existed. Temperatures fluctuated rapidly from one extreme to another.

Compared to the warm, shallow waters in which all kinds of organisms could flourish, land was downright hostile. But if you were a photosynthetic organism, it did offer some pretty big incentives. For one, you could take in direct sunlight, unfiltered by water. And for another, carbon dioxide −□ plant food −□ was plentiful.

These incentives, it seems, were enough for green algae, the very first plants, to migrate onto land. The reason they were able to survive? Fungi. We don't know how fungi and algae originally came together −□ but we do know they quickly formed an inseparable bond. These alliances between plants and fungi are known as mycorrhizal relationships, and more than 90 percent of all modern plant species depend on them to survive.

The key message is this: Mycorrhizal relationships are the bedrock of life on Earth.

Mycorrhizal relationships work like this: Plants use photosynthesis to harvest carbon from the atmosphere and convert it into sugars and fats, which they in turn pass along to fungi. In return, super-fine mycorrhizal hyphae scavenge for water and minerals in nooks and crannies that plant roots can't reach.

Some species of plants and fungi make better bedmates than others, though. Certain mycorrhizal fungi are stingy and like to "hoard" nutrients like phosphorus. Others are

27

cooperative, sharing their phosphorus at all times.

But that's not all. Different fungi can have major impacts on various plant characteristics. Two similar experiments tested the effects of different fungal communities on strawberry plants. Interestingly, some made the fruit taste sweeter. Others made the plants produce more berries. Some even made plants more attractive to bumblebees.

And mycorrhizal relationships don't just have an impact on crops. They're also essential for keeping our climate stable.

Three to four hundred million years ago, plants had spread across the world and evolved into larger and more complex forms. As they grew taller and wider, they sucked a whopping 90 percent of the atmosphere's carbon into their bodies. The dramatic drop in atmospheric carbon triggered a period of global cooling.

Fungi contributed to this new and more temperate climate. By providing plants with phosphorus, which is abundant in soil, they aided plants in their prolific growth. Without fungi,☐ life as we know it might never have come to be.

FUNGI, PLANTS, BACTERIA, AND TREES ARE CONNECTED VIA "WOOD WIDE WEBS.

The Pacific Northwest is home to lush, green forests. But among the thickets of vibrant emerald, in the shadiest parts of the forest, small patches of stark white plants can be found pushing up from the ground.

These plants, known as "ghost pipes," are the species Monotropa uniflora. Unlike most plants, they don't have the ability to photosynthesize –□ and thus they have no leaves or green coloring. But if they can't photosynthesize, how do they survive?

In short, Monotropa depends entirely on fungi, making it what's known as a mycoheterotroph. These types of organisms receive all the carbon and nutrients they need from fungi. But they give nothing back in return. The mystery of this curious, seemingly one-sided relationship reveals a vast, interconnected web of mycorrhizal networks hidden beneath the soil.

Here's the key message: Fungi, plants, bacteria, and trees are connected via "wood wide webs."

Much of the time, plants and fungi share carbon and nutrients using a private mycorrhizal network. But mycorrhizal networks can also be shared between two different plants. This is the case with Monotropa. Green plants are able to take in carbon; then, they transfer it to Monotropa via a shared fungal highway.

And mycorrhizal networks can be shared by more than two plants. In fact, these networks can connect a vast expanse of trees, bacteria, and plants through which hormones, toxins, nitrogen, and water can be transported.

Mycorrhizal networks bring to mind the architecture of another network: the World Wide Web. For that reason, shared mycorrhizal networks are often referred to as "wood wide webs." By "hacking" into this web, mycoheterotrophs are able to survive.

The concept of the wood wide web is illustrative. But it also reeks of plant-centrism, depicting plants as the main nodes in the network. Fungi are organisms with their own self-interest in mind, too —□ so why would they settle for a mere supporting role?

Let's instead imagine that fungi are in charge. This would make sense —□ after all,□ keeping up relationships with multiple plants means fungi can continue to survive even if one of the plants dies. And there is more than one kind of wood wide web —□ in some, fungi exist only to consume plants, not nourish them. From a myco-centric perspective, wood wide webs are regular fungal networks in which plants and trees just happen to be entangled.

THE WAY WE PERCEIVE FUNGI REVEALS A LOT ABOUT US.

You might be familiar with Carl Linnaeus's famous system of taxonomy, which sorts organisms into different categories. But did you know it was only designed to classify plants and animals? Fungi, it turns out, are neither. Yet fungi weren't assigned to their own distinct kingdom until the mid-1960s.

Given their many strange and unique genetic traits, fungi often defy classification. Despite this, humans are constantly trying to shoehorn them into categories we ourselves invented. Might there be a better way to make sense of fungi?

The key message here is: The way we perceive fungi reveals a lot about us.

A researcher named Toby Kiers studies the ways in which plants and fungi maintain their balance of power. By using radioactive labels and special light-emitting tags, Kiers traces the paths of carbon and phosphorus between plants and fungi. But how does each organism manage that exchange?

From one angle, it can be seen as a complex economic trade, in which plants and fungi engage in trade-offs and compromises. For instance, Kiers found that in parts of a mycelial network where phosphorus is scarce, plants pay a higher "price" for the phosphorus. In other words, they give more carbon to the fungi for every unit of phosphorus they receive. Meanwhile, in areas where phosphorus is plentiful, fungi receive a worse "price" —□ that is, less carbon in exchange for each unit of phosphorus.

In this way, fungi seem to operate according to the rules of a kind of market, or stock exchange. We can view them as economic investors — capitalistic "Wall Street" fungi, so to speak. But this doesn't quite tell the whole story —□ and perhaps it's more telling of how we see ourselves than the way fungi actually operate.

When plants and fungi engage in symbiosis, for instance, we might just as easily view it as an example of a functioning socialist society, in which wealth is redistributed. Green plants don't need to supply carbon for free to their mycoheterotrophic cousins, yet they do it anyway.

Are plants and fungi fundamentally cooperative or competitive? Are they mutualistic or parasitic? The answer may depend on your cultural background or political views. Metaphors and analogies like these can help us understand fungi, but they can also distort our perception of them. Perhaps, instead, we should embrace the uncertainties that fungi present us with and study them on their own terms.

FUNGI OFFER POTENTIAL SOLUTIONS TO ENVIRONMENTAL PROBLEMS.

It's no secret that fungi have voracious appetites –□ some more so than others.

Pleurotus mycelium, which fruits into edible oyster mushrooms, is especially omnivorous. If presented with a smorgasbord of used diapers, for instance, Pleurotus will dine happily. In one experiment, Pleurotus was able to reduce a collection of diapers to 15 percent of its original mass in two months.

There are some things Pleurotus won't normally eat –□ like cigarette butts, which are saturated with toxic residues. However, some experiments have shown that it may be possible to train Pleurotus to eat these toxic substances by weaning the fungus off of other food sources.

Pleurotus could be unleashed on agricultural waste to improve air quality and reduce the amount of biomass we thermally combust. Other fungi can be used to consume and clean up radioactive waste, neurotoxins, pesticides, explosives like TNT, and even some plastics.

This is the key message: Fungi offer potential solutions to environmental problems.

Fungi's unique skills are highly useful for breaking down pollutants, a process called mycoremediation. They also demonstrate great promise in mycofabrication −□ a creative process rather than a destructive one.

Just take the American company Ecovative Design, which makes building materials from mycelium. Mycelial foam can be used to replace heavily polluting building materials, while mycelial leather can replace animal leather. There are other upsides, too: mycelial products can be grown in less than a week, and they can even be composted at the end of their lives.

Fungal solutions can also be applied to improve health in humans and many other organisms. The antibiotic penicillin is perhaps the best-known example. But mycologist Paul Stamets is also working on a fungal compound designed for honeybees. Global agriculture depends heavily on pollination from bees, but their populations are declining. One of the culprits behind this is the varroa mite – a parasite that sucks fluid from bees' bodies and can transmit a variety of deadly viruses. But wood-rotting fungi, a rich source of antiviral compounds, can be administered to bees to dramatically reduce their susceptibility to many of these diseases.

Of course, lab experiments aren't always representative of how things will work out in the field. But one thing is certain: humanity faces environmental catastrophe from many sides. Agricultural production has plateaued and temperatures are rising while toxic waste piles up.

If we hope to survive, the future may well be fungal.

KEY NOTE.

The key message in these read:

Fungi are remarkable organisms whose contributions to life on Earth have been essential –☐ yet go largely unnoticed. The abilities of fungi are wide-ranging and extraordinary: lichens can thrive in extreme temperatures, truffles can produce an irresistible smell, and psilocybin mushrooms can induce visions that ultimately improve human mental health. In the future, collaboration with fungi may allow humanity to solve its most pressing issues, including reducing pollution, cleaning up waste, and improving agriculture.

Printed in Great Britain
by Amazon

55216943R00025